Paw Prints on My Heart

Furry, Feathery and Scaly Poems

by Mary Beth Magee

BOTR Press, Poplarville, MS

All rights reserved. No part of this book may be used or reproduced by any means, graphic, electronic or mechanical, including photocopying, recording, taping or by any information storage electrical system without the written permission of the author except in the case of brief quotations embodied in critical articles and review.

Copyright 2024   Mary Beth Magee
Published by BOTR Press, Poplarville, MS

Cover image by Mary Beth Magee using
Clip art by GDJ, TimLesch and Woofer
Interior graphics by Mary Beth Magee
From a design by Tialosi
All from openclipart.com

This is a work of original poetry written by the author. All rights are reserved.

ISBN: 978-1-7378103-4-6

Paw Prints on My Heart

Furry, Feathery and Scaly Poems

Table of Contents

Welcome	1
Canine Capers: It's a Dog's Life	3
Dog Tales	5
Puppy Ears	6
Boys and Dogs and James H Street	7
Blue Dog Blues	8
The Rescue	9
Puppy Tails	10
Sentinel	11
Fifty Words for Puppy	12
Multiple Personalities	13
Feline Follies: Who Runs the House?	15
Disappearing Act	17
Alley, Alley, All in Free	18
The Bookstore Cat	19
A Cat Named Stu	20
Emerald Orbs	21
The Clever Kitten	22
Jacques Edmund	23
The Panther	24
Insect Images: Wings and More	25
Dragonfly Alibis	27
The Visitor	28
Dragonflies	29
Draped in Pearls	30
Butterflies	31
The Parsley Thief	32

Taking Wing: Come Fly With Me	33
Pelican Power	35
Feathered Flood	36
Ruby Wings	37
A Haiku for Puffins	38
Puffins	39
Into the Wild: Who's Watching Who?	41
Cougar Encounter	43
Living with Nature	44
Southern Beauty	46
The Symphony	47
Little Armadillo	48
Porch Dragon	49
The Rope	50
Serpentine	51
Dinner Bell!	51
Saddle Up!	52
One Golden Horse	53
Spooky	54
A Haiku for Zebras	56
Zebra Stripes	57
Cares and Fears	58
Bear in the Woods	59
The Herd	60
Thank You	61
Poetry Books by Mary Beth Magee	63
Index by Poetic Forms	64
Index by Title	66

Dedicated to all animals everywhere and to the people who love them.
May the partnership go on forever.

Welcome

Our world is blessed with a wide assortment of animals in all shapes and sizes. The sheer variety staggers my mind.

Some are pets, part of our family and household. Whether we choose them or they choose us doesn't matter. They leave their impression on our lives, however long they stay. Hence, the title of this collection, Paw Prints on My Heart.

Others remain independent, whether seen often or only once. Even wild things can leave an indelible heart impression.

You will find examples of both domestic and wild creatures on these pages. Some have fur, some have scales, others have feathers. Each of them touched me in some way. I hope they will touch you as well.

Thank you for visiting this crazy world of critters I inhabit. Enjoy your visit.

Mary Beth Magee

Poplarville, MS

June 2024

Canine Capers:
It's a Dog's Life!

Dog Tales

Dogs

Bark,

Tails wag,

As they chase

Butterfly shadows

Across sun-dappled parks and yards,

Joyously playing canine games with nature's free toys.

Leaping skyward, launching like rockets breaking
    free of earth's gravity they fly on wings

Of exuberant happiness, airborne, weightless, free.

Running, panting, catching nothing

But mouthfuls of sun,

They live lives

Of dog

Dreams

Won.

Puppy Ears

Most pups have ears which fit their little heads.
But some are tasked with wing-like hearing parts.
They drag them from their food bowls to their beds
And forward progress make in fits and starts.

A head shake sends ours tumbling cross the room,
Like crumpled paper rolling on the wind.
You might think puppy's met his final doom.
But no, he has done nothing of the kind.

A wriggle then a tiny little yelp,
Four paws beneath his body realigned.
He hears the siren call of kibble's smell
And seeks the kitchen, one thing on his mind.

Ears hide the bowl from me, but not from pup.
He roots past them and so begins to sup.

Boys and Dogs and James H Street

Boys and dogs and polliwogs filled his stories.
He wrote of southern dreams and childhood perspectives,
Some of them true,
Some not exactly true in fact, but accurate in spirit.
James Howell Street wrote them as he saw them,
Rascals, heroes and all, documenting southern culture.
From little Lumberton, Mississippi to the world's stage he trod
Recounting the perceived heart of his South and its past.
He told of hunters and their companions,
Colorful whirls of feathers as birds flushed from cover,
Faithful dogs retrieving felled targets,
Free-spirited women and unorthodox men.
He wrote too of history as seen through his own eyes.
Magazines helped to spread his tales,
Sharing a biscuiteater and a barkless Basenji,
Small boys and old men,
Clever, kindly women and countless other rich characters
With a world starving for great stories told well.
Each idiosyncrasy, each foible came to life in colorful fashion.
He told of those who worked the land or lived off the land,
And those who loved them.
Sometimes Hollywood called, seeking fodder for filmmaker's art.
Even in that medium, the stories still shone.
His work highlighted a long ago world, imperfect—yes,
Unfair—often, Southern—definitely.
Society may label his portfolio as less than politically correct, but
His stories examined characters and eccentricities
While gently highlighting the social issues.
His unvarnished images may ruffle some
But others will delight to visit the south in its rich detail,
Filled with swamps and woods and farmland,
Peopled with boys and dogs and polliwogs.

 # Blue Dog Blues

(Inspired by *"Blue Dog"* by George Rodrigue)

Blue dog,
You sit and you watch.
The world goes by
And some see you.

Others don't notice
Your blue presence.
Some smile, some scowl,
Some giggle in delight.

Blue dog,
Are you blue because you are sad?
If you played an instrument
Would it be a cool blues horn?

Or are you blue because
Your thoughts are flying high,
Roving space and time
While humans hurry by?

Blue dog,
You sit and you watch.
I wish I could read
Your blue dog mind.

You seem so wise,
Taking in the world.
Or are you simply
Laughing at us all?

The Rescue

Some called her a rescue dog.
True, I adopted her from the local humane society.
The only home she had ever known was gone,
Her previous owner taken to a nursing home.
I found her there,
Huddled in a concrete-floored run,
Matted, tangled, with an overgrown coat,
And no eyes, it seemed, hidden under her bangs.
Truth to tell, she wasn't much to see.
My heart ached for this little ink blot curled up on the floor.
She stood and crept to the gate where I stood.
Neck stretched out, she sniffed my hand.
I must have passed her test because she inched closer.
The tiniest pink tongue I had ever seen on a dog licked my fingers
Through the cold metal of the run,
And I was helpless to leave her.
Bathed, clipped and groomed, she proved to be
A beautiful miniature schnauzer,
Jet black but for a narrow white blaze on her chest,
With intelligent obsidian eyes revealed by the groomer's art.
She felt soft and warm, and offered multiple affectionate cuddles.
Sitting beside me as I studied toward my long delayed degree,
She inched ever further into my lap
As though to study with me.
Some might call her a rescue dog,
The plain truth is, she rescued me
From loneliness and the grief of a failed marriage.
She brought me joy and hope and a reason to live.
We rescued each other and shared our lives and love
For the rest of her life.

Puppy Tails

Puppy tails
Wagging with delight
Wreak havoc!

Honorable Mention, Wombat Award,

Mississippi Poetry Society 2023

Sentinel

He is not my dog by ownership,
But oh, he has claimed my heart.
The next door neighbor's mixed breed
Was quite wild at the start.
He'd wander over, stay a while,
In a half-grown puppy way.
No manners yet, but mad to please
He learned some more each day.
One morning as I left for work,
He blocked me from the stairs.
Gaze fixed in the distance,
He growled and snarled with glares
At something he perceived as threat.
He would not let me pass.
Then suddenly he sat and wagged
His tail, content at last.
My sentinel protected me -
From what, I could not say.
But he is even more dear to me
Ever since that day.

 # Fifty Words for Puppy

Give me fifty words for puppy, if you think you can:
1 Puppy, 2 Canine-Ette, 3 FakeyFierceness,
4 Toothymouth, 5 PiddlePuddlePot, 6 Furry,
7 LickyLaughterGiver, 8 Knotty, 9 BallChaser
10 BarfBucket,

(And forty more, and forty more, and forty more to find!)
11 FurBallOnFeet, 12 MobileWarmth, 13 ChewingShoes,
14 WhimperWhispers, 15 DogToBe, 16 AllTeeth,
17 SmileySnuggler, 18 SurrogateChild, 19 ColdWetNose,

(Find thirty-one more, can't you, can't you, can't you?)
20 SockChomper, 21 BarkyBreath, 22 FuzzyAlarmClock,
23 LapWarmer, 24 GrowlARama,
25 EarCleaner, 26 WhiningWiggle,
27 FurBaby, 28 LittleClawsPaws, 29 ShredderSpectaculaire,
30 TailSlapping,

(Just two handsful more, not much, just two handsful)
31 TreatChomper, 32 StickRetriever, 33 Pup-a-Palooza
34 SuperKlutzKid, 35 Woofer-No Tweeter, I 36 PilferPillow
37 WriggleWiggleWag, 38 CookieThief, 39 BratDog,
40 GrowIntoPaws, 41 PeriodicPainInTheButkis, 42 BestBuddy,

(Almost there, if you care, just eight more if you dare)
43 ComeHereRightNow! 44 WalkRacer, 45 PuppyPawPrints, ,
46 BlessedAndBlessing, 47 MuddyFeet, 48 WannabeWolf,
49 FourLeggedNanny
(Just one left now, just one and you've won!)

50 Puppy-GrownTooSoon (sadly sigh).

(Inspired by "Fifty Words for Snow" by Kate Bush)

Multiple Personalities

(inspired by *"We Stand Together"* by George Rodrigue)

I thought I knew you, Blue Dog. In art books you reside.

In calendars and souvenirs for sale you're known to hide.

But in the Sculpture Garden, I see you're not so mellow.

You have a flaming red aspect. Another one is yellow.

These different faces prompt me to ask you to decide,

Are you a cool or bright dog or a hot dog deep inside?

Feline Follies: Who Runs the House?

Disappearing Act

A moment ago, I saw you there.
Now you are gone, and I don't know where.
A caramel blur and scratching skid
Marked the disappearing act you did.
Is hide and go seek your favorite game?
Maybe I am the one I should blame.
I only wanted to hold you close
But you prefer freedom. Adios,
Until you get hungry or want a treat.
That's when I'll see your caramel feet
Making their way from your hiding spot.
And I'll gladly give you what I've got.
Sweet kitten, you're safe here by my side.
One day you'll see there's no need to hide.
Your disappearing act you can lose.
To make your home here I hope you'll choose.

Alley, Alley, All in Free

He's an alley cat, gray and striped and tough.
No walls to hold him. He likes living rough.
Prowling and yowling, he struts through the town.
Over the fences, up one street and down
The other he moves. His tail waving high,
He seeks out his tribute while passing by.
A bowl of milk here, a bit of fish there,
A bite of a sandwich stolen with care.
And when he finds one, a rat tastes just fine.
He isn't picky on where he might dine.
Some curse him, some laud him. He pays no mind.
Gray tiger stalking, the king of his kind.
He's untamed, unfettered. No house cat, he.
A symbol of independence. He's free.

The Bookstore Cat

The smoky-gray cat lurks high on a shelf,
Watching each patron with indolent care.
No one knows where she came from or how long
She's stayed. The cat has just always been there.
With pretty white boots, a shirtfront to match,
Such a picture of feline perfection.
For decades it seems, she's kept careful watch
On the shop and its handpicked selections.
Bestsellers she picks by tapping her paw
On the cover. No one knows how she knows.
"Agatha's Choice" read the signs in the shop,
Each book marked by Agatha's dainty toes.
No one can sway her, though many have tried
With catnip and salmon to tempt her taste.
A ghost cat eats nothing (in this world, that is)
So their efforts have sadly gone to waste.
The Bookstore Cat's haunts haven't changed with time
Though the owners and contents may vary.
She still rules the shelves in the friendly shop.
She's the ghost cat who's cozy, not scary.
Come for a visit and stay for awhile.
Let her pick out a book for your pleasure.
The Bookstore Cat-Agatha-waits for you
There. She's a cat you surely will treasure.

Previously published in *Felines and Phantoms*, 2024

A Cat Named Stu

He called her Stupid Cat –
The stray on the carport,
Royally reclining in a patch of sunshine.
Exactly where the car should be parked, she napped.
"Get out of there, Stupid Cat," he yelled,
And chased her away.
She came back.
Day after day, she returned.
Day after day, he called her "Stupid Cat"
And chased her away once again.
One day, she slipped into the apartment through the
    opened door
As we carried in groceries.
She made herself at home.
Not such a Stupid Cat at all.
Perfectly mannered, quietly elegant she
Soon ruled her two-bedroom castle
With a benevolent heart.
I changed her name to Stu
And told her it was short for Stupendous Cat.
She nodded,
Purred her agreement
And took a nap.

Third Place, Purrfectly Pleasing Pets,
Mississippi Poetry Society SpringFest 2023

Emerald Orbs

There is strange new entity
Threatening my identity.
Where once I called my house my own,
I find I now am not alone.
Twin green globes peer out and blink
From underneath the kitchen sink,
Or from the darkness 'neath my bed.
From a face on an ebon' head
These emerald orbs watch my routine
As I read, or I cook or clean.
Like a cop on a stakeout they
Note my every move through the day.
My kitten will one day relax.
For now, I ply her with food and snacks,
Aiming to win her affection.
The emerald orbs make inspection
Of my world. I hope she'll decide,
Once she's made the effort and tried,
That she fits in and likes it here.
My emerald orbed kitten, so dear.

The Clever Kitten

The precious kitten showed up on my step that day.
Soft gray fur, white boots and bib, so small.
I thought to ease her hunger in a kindly way.
She ate it up with no delay at all.
Poor kitten, with her ribs revealed by hunger
And sadness in her dark eyes, broke my heart.
Another can of tuna, I shouldn't wonder
Would help her energize for a new start.
'Twas only seven meals I gave the kitten.
She blossomed like a rose in summer's sun.
And only after I was firmly smitten
Did I then grasp the giant thing I'd done.
For kitten was a missus and a mama.
Her flower was a litter 'neath my stair.
Not one, but four new felines bring me drama
As her babies join her in my care.

Third Place, Fast and Furryous Award,
Mississippi Poetry Society SpringFest 2023

Jacques Edmund

Of all the kittens, he was the smallest—
The runt, by any definition.
He was the kitten marked like his mama.
He inherited her sweet disposition,
But not her timidity. He dared
To fight his siblings for Mama's supply.
He was first out to explore from the birthing bed.
There seemed to be nothing he wouldn't try.
He would climb any height put before him,
Be it sofa or bedspread or knee.
From there he would dive headfirst on his way
Like a cliff diver seeking the sea.
I called him Jacques Edmund, which seemed to fit.
He seemed modeled on two special men:
Jacques Cousteau, who explored the oceans' depths,
Edmund Hillary, who climbed the earth's mountains.
Once the others were weaned and off to new homes,
My runt had a good chance to grow.
Another frontier conquered by Jacques Edmund,
The greatest adventurer I know!

The Panther

(Inspired by detail from Walter Anderson's Little Room)

The mighty hunter stalks his domain,
Weaving through grassy wilds unknown.
His green eyes examine strange terrain
And claim the prey there as his own.
In his own heart, he is the master
Of the wild world he knows so well.
This feline's realm spreads wilder, vaster
Than any human tongue can tell.
See him as only a small black cat,
And miss the mighty heart within.
He does not see his own world as flat,
But tall, mysterious, arcane.
When the great hunter's day has ended
He'll go back to the place he rules,
Secure in knowing he has tended
To life, with tooth and claw his tools.

Insect Images: Wings and More

Dragonfly Alibis

I watched as the bright blue body
Of a dragonfly leapt from a leaf,
Propelled by gossamer wings,
Darting quick as a breath,
Intent on an unlucky mosquito.
In a flash of blue,
Winged death struck the insect
As the heroic dragonfly
Captured and devoured
The sting-y pest.
Some might call this murder
Of a poor defenseless insect.
I call it a service to mankind.
This dragonfly needs no alibi
To clear his name in court.
He committed justifiable homicide,
Protecting humanity.
He deserves a medal with his meal.

The Visitor

You visit for a moment,
Accept a breath of hospitality,
Then dash away again.
You share your company briefly.

But in that time, oh,
The magic you bring.
From tiny eggs to instars
To gloriously patterned wing.

I watched you hatch and crawl,
Grow, shed and wriggle.
You change your dress. Your
New look makes me giggle.

You give me joy and delight
With your aerial ballet.
My royal friend, magician,
Harlequin at play,

Dear monarch, share your gift
Of grand, exuberant joy
With all. Give us eyes to
See, and feelings to employ.

You set an example
Of living in the moment.
Let us live so our days
Are likewise spent.

Dash on, my friend,
Your destiny calls.
Send your children my way
When the milkweed grows tall.

Dragonflies

Dragonflies buzz around the garden
Iridescent splendor on the wing.
So many jewel-toned bodies sailing
On gossamer lace over the flower beds.
Which colors dance most vibrantly?
Do the dragonflies' hues outshine
The flowers curtsying in the gentle breezes
Or do the bright flowers' shades dull
The dragonflies' darting flashes on the zephyr winds?
The blossoms may wave their leaves, claiming
"Me, me!"
But they will fade and fall in short order,
Petals browning on the ground,
Rejoining the earth from which they sprang.
The dragonflies will disappear, too,
Flying away to another garden,
Carried out of my sight on the breeze
To another insect banquet.
I know they have only a few weeks
To pursue their winged dream but
In my mind's eye, they remain forever
Bright as a king's ransom,
Glittering in the sunshine
As they buzz around another garden.

Draped in Pearls

(Inspired by "Be Dazzled" by Charla Bullard)

I crept, Cinderella-like, up the walk
Through the garden to the front door
No shoes lost, but still a fairy-tale experience
In my receding memory.
Too much wine, too much dancing,
Too much time spent at the ball
Moving among the beautiful people.
The sun accused me of my misbehavior
As it climbed over the horizon.
But I fingered a strand of the pearls draped round my neck,
Smiled my brightest smile and
Twirled at the foot of the stairs.
"I had fun," I whispered.
"I was beautiful, garbed in my sapphire blue gown
And draped in my pearls.
I was almost the belle of the ball."
When my joyful pirouette ended,
I found myself face to face with a miracle.
A golden silk orb-weaver spider had been hard at work
And her beautiful web shimmered with dew-drop gems
In the early morning light.
I may have been draped in pearls,
But her intricate web was draped in diamonds,
Brilliant, glittering diamonds fitting the queen of the garden.
I curtsied in homage to her,
A humble member of her court honoring her presence.

Finalist, 2024 Tishomingo Arts Council
Ekphrastic Poetry Contest

Butterflies

Can you see them dancing in the sunlight,
Graceful wings sweeping the sunbeams clean
Of dust and pollen, hate and negative energy?
The beautiful butterflies fill the world with love.

Graceful wings sweeping the sunbeams clean,
They brighten the landscape like jewelry
Hung with colorful crystals to cleanse the very air

Of dust and pollen, hate and negative energy.
The variety of colors and patterns they bring
Offer us a glimpse of something much bigger than ourselves.

The beautiful butterflies fill the world with love
And teach us of the value of the most fragile lives.
May they ever fill our vision with their sunshine dance.

The Parsley Thief

She inches her way up the delicate stem,
Black and yellow stripes undulating
Against a green background as she moves
Along the path to tender leaves of parsley.
An intruder in my herb garden,
She ignores my presence.
With singular intent and laser focus,
She pursues a meal at my expense.
I try to remove her with a gentle scooping,
But she responds with angry orange horns waving.
Should I wreak vengeance
On this colorful intruder to save my crop?
But if I do, there will be one less beautiful
Black swallowtail butterfly in the world.
So, I will plant extra parsley,
And make my herbal donation to
The future of the species which graces the sky
Over my garden
And blesses my day.

Taking Wing:
Come Fly with Me

Pelican Power

I've always loved the pelican,
Clown prince of coastal birds.
He fills his pouch with lunchtime fish,
Funny beyond all words.

Ungainly as he launches,
But graceful as he flies,
He waddles by on beach and wharf
But pirouettes through skies.

A somber, judge-like fellow,
As he surveys the coast.
And dives in for his fishing
Where he thinks he'll catch the most.

Sometimes he sits in dignity
Upon a brine-soaked piling.
I may be wrong, but oftentimes
It looks as though he's smiling.

There is a certain elegance
Found in his solo stance.
Perhaps he is a wallflower,
Just waiting for a chance

To ask a lady pelican
To join him in a flight.
If he should ask politely,
Who knows? Perhaps she might.

I wish you well, Sir Pelican.
May fair winds lift your wings.
And thank you for the many smiles
Your charming presence brings.

Feathered Flood

At the sound of a cascade of feed pellets
And cracked corn ringing a dinner bell
Against the weathered metal feeder,
The feathered flood poured forth.
Hens and half-grown chicks
In a yellow-gold tsunami
Punctuated by darker flamboyances
Of red and brown tail feathers
Arching backward in a cascade
Flooded the coop floor.
The lone rooster in the pen
Strutted from his perch to the feeder,
Scattering the earliest arrivals.
The splash of water pouring into the trough
Distracted the harried hens
From his high-handed demeanor.
Like commuters in a busy transit station,
The birds dashed back and forth
Across the dirt floor,
A tide rising and ebbing around
The islands of food and water.
While they flowed between their basic needs,
I raided their nests for eggs for my breakfast,
The gift of the feathered flood.

Ruby Wings

Winter has drained the world of color,
Leaving only drab grays and browns behind.
The garden, once lush and verdant,
Now displays only sticks and stubs.
Even the birds seem colorless.
Mourning doves and mockingbirds swoop and swirl
Against the cloud-scudded sky.
The sun hides for another day,
Unwilling to face the chilly land.
When I feel as though the world is lost
And cheer cannot be found,
A sudden burst of color arrives.
Scarlet against the drab canvas,
A cardinal soars to a naked branch,
Red as blood, bright as flame,
Cocky as any peacock in his apparel.
His ruby wings flutter into place.
Can any bird break winter's gray hold
As brilliantly as a male cardinal?

A Haiku for Puffins

Like small monks in prayer
Puffins cross the rocky land -
Fish within their mouths

Puffins

As nature's clowns the darling puffins rule.
Black clad, with white shirtfront they face the world
Formally dressed. They dive with wings well furled
To splash into a fish-filled dining pool.

Avian Pagliacci, losing ground
To changes crowding close upon your shore,
You struggle to survive. With nothing more
Than clumsy charm and precious face so round

You slip into our hearts, then fly away
To seek your meal or build a nesting place.
I cannot stop the smile upon my face
Each time I think of you. You light my day!

I wish you well, dear puffin - sweet-faced clown!
For causing regal smiles, you've earned a crown!

Into the Wild: Who's Watching Who?

Cougar Encounter

Tawny, stealthy,

I watch the monster approach

From my hidden vantage point.

Too big a foe to challenge to fight.

In regal disdain, I step out and stare,

Meeting oversized eyes with cool boldness.

I deem it no threat,

Turn my face from the creature.

With a flip of my tail, I walk away,

Unscathed.

Living with nature

Living with nature carries certain wonderful benefits,
But also many challenges.
Once upon a time, the peaceful pond held fish.
Small-mouth bass, catfish, and bream
Swam there and grew there,
Lived and mated there,
Fought there and were caught there.
An occasional snake or two lived there, too,
Gliding in shallow elegant s-shapes
Across the glassy surface of the pond.
They avoided human contact,
Having no interest in creatures too big for a meal,
And so, they caused no fuss.
Then came the turtles,
Big snappers which preyed on young fish
And threatened swimmers' toes and fingers.
The shelled critter count climbed
As the finned critter count declined.
They defied our best efforts at
Eradication, and decimated the fish population.
One day, a lodge appeared in the pond,
Sticks and mud packed into a messy dome
Which rose just above the water level.
A beaver family announced their presence
With clogged culverts and felled saplings,
And even fewer fish.
This spring, a new visitor signed in-
A young alligator, gliding just beneath the surface,
Only nostrils and eyeballs visible.
The beaver are gone,
Either ousted or eaten
By the new occupant.

The frog population has plummeted.
No one swims in the pond anymore.
Watching the progression,
I fear what might be next.

I can promise this much…
If I spot a dorsal fin cutting the water,
I'm gone!

Southern Beauty

Have you ever seen the sun dance on a bayou?
Or watched a hummingbird's darting flight?
Has a garter snake disturbed your peaceful strolling?
Have you laughed as fireflies played at twilight?

No music can compare to summer breezes
Whisp'ring through magnolia trees and pines.
No blanket can out-cover verdant kudzu
As it drapes itself o'er fence and power lines.

If you've napped to lazy drone of tawny honeybees,
Or wakened to the song of summer's rain,
Then you've had a taste of southern beauty.
Its lure will ever call you back again.

The Symphony

Late in the evening, the music starts.
I only have to step out on the porch
To hear the free concert.
The bullfrogs down at the pond
Start the song
With a rich melody filling the air.
Smaller frogs join in,
An amphibious chorus accompanying.
Then the crickets, scattered around the garden,
Add the harmony line, rhythmically soaring
Around the score.
Just when I think
The music can't become any more beautiful,
An owl provides the bass line as he questions
"Who" is listening to their concert.
The answer is simple. Me!

Little Armadillo

He's just a little armadillo,
    living way down in the south.
He has a pointed little nose, and
    a long tongue in his mouth.
He carries his own house with him
    like a little banded camper.
He looks so funny when he walks.
    He scuffles, he can't scamper.
He'll eat the bugs and varmints
    which he finds down in the dirt.
And fruits and seeds are yummy.
    He will have them for dessert!
The nine bands laid out on his shell
    cause him to look quite dashing.
But don't mistake him for a pet.
    His claws are good for slashing,
And when it comes to digging,
    armadillos have a knack.
He's just a little armadillo,
    with his house upon his back.

Porch Dragon

He poses in solemn dignity there on the back porch.
Black and tan chevrons mark his regal robes.
A steady glare from obsidian eyes
Challenges me to move;
Surely, he would bolt if I did.
Dear dragon, I only wish
To fill my eyes with your magnificence.
I mean you no harm.
A twitch of your tail tells me
You are restless,
Ready to move on
To some less trafficked sundrenched site.
Pray, wait a moment.
Let me capture your splendor with my camera
And thus preserve a precious moment.
As I snap the shutter,
My dragon blinks at me as if to say,
"Thank you for thinking me so grand
Though I am but a poor fence swift."
And he is gone, with a flick of his tail.
He leaves me with only a photo and a memory
Of my back porch dragon.

The Rope

Bags of groceries balanced equally between my two hands, I headed from my car to the red brick summit of the back porch steps.

Careful of your footing, I told myself as I crossed the yard, watching the ground as I walked to be sure of my stability. I paused at the first step to catch my breath, ready to ascend. From the corner of my eye, I spotted a piece of old gnarled rope, green with a blue tinge, like verdigris on well-aged copper. It lay close to the stems of a spreading Indian Hawthorn bush in the garden beside the porch. *Who threw a piece of rope in among the flowers?* I wondered. *I'll have to pick it up when I've gotten all the groceries in the house.*

With my attention now focused on the rope, I moved one foot onto the lowest step and froze in midmotion. *Why, that rope has eyes!*

I looked closer. What I had perceived as discolored rope fibers were scales covering the length of a Mississippi green water snake. It seemed to be wrapped around the base of the bush. I gazed at the graceful reptile, the better to appreciate its bluish-green beauty.

It seemed to feel my gaze. Alas, alerted to my presence the snake bolted, gone in a fluid sage motion around the end of the porch. I do hope it will come to visit again.

Serpentine

Surrounded by little boys in Cub Scout uniforms,
I stood, frozen, anxiety-riddled. Terrified.
The young man behind the table held a hog nosed snake.
One by one, my young charges touched it,
Stroked it, held it, commented on it.
My stomach clenched as one of them offered it to me.
Would it turn up in my bedroll if I refused?
I steeled myself and accepted the offer.
The snake wrapped its tail around my arm,
Velvet smooth and gently caressing.
It turned wise, ancient eyes upon me.
Did we commune in that moment?
Did the snake impart some secret serenity?
I only know my terror was gone,
Replaced by wonder and appreciation
For the beautiful magic of a hog nosed snake.

Dinner Bell!

Gecko on window,
Bug in sight.
Dine and dash lizard.

Saddle Up!

I swung up into the saddle
Feeling every dream come true.
This moment I had prayed for
Had finally come due.

Two decades I had fantasized
And wondered if I could
Ever truly ride a horse.
Given the chance, I would

Fly across the land as one
With a trusty, loving steed.
The money for the horse and tack
And stable and vet care and feed

Were far beyond my means.
My dream seemed far away,
A fantasy, at best,
Left for another day.

When the call came to me
I finally had my chance
A friend invited me to join the ride.
It was a great new experience.

One Golden Horse

Scarlet saddle blanket rests soft and plush,
'Neath leather saddle trimmed with silver, lush.
One golden horse, with flowing cloud-white mane.
Provides a perfect throne for a temporary queen.

And thus, an earth-bound woman can be freed
From gravity's demand, to fly on such a steed.
I feel muscles, piston-like, expand and contract
Beneath me as we exercise our mystic pact.

For just a moment, we two distinct creatures
Meld to form a single being, strong and sure.
Horse and rider, gliding, flying – one.
As fast as the wind, and bright as any sun,

Too soon the magic ended – we had to part.
No distance can remove you from my heart,
As memory permits me to return.
For golden days, one golden horse, I yearn.

Spooky

She called him Spooky, a dramatic Appaloosa
With white rings around his pale eyes.
A new addition to the boarding stable, he greeted her
Each time she went to feed her horses.
He wasn't hers, but he acted as if he was.
They would engage in conversations –
She'd tell him how beautiful he was.
And he would agree,
Bobbing his head and nickering softly.
Most of the horses there were good-natured,
But she was warned of one – a real bad actor.
"Watch out for Brandy," the stable owner cautioned.
"He bites, he kicks, he's just plain bad news."
So, she promised never to mess with him —
A promise easily kept since she'd never seen him on this corridor.
One day, as she went through the stable on the way to her horses,
Spooky stuck his head out to greet her as usual.
She scratched behind his ear as he nuzzled her hair,
Then patted his neck prior to continuing on to her tasks.
A heavy hand grabbed her shoulder.
She whirled around, ready to defend herself.
"Are you crazy? That horse could kill you!"
The stable owner seemed distressed to the point of distraction.
"Who? Spooky? He wouldn't hurt me. We're friends," she answered.
"His name isn't Spooky, it's Brandy
And he's put three people in the hospital.
His own master can't ride him."

"That's impossible. He's a sweetheart.
He's never so much as snorted at me in all the months I've known him."
The stable owner shook his head.
"You have no idea how lucky you've been."
But she knew the truth. She hadn't known to be afraid of him
So, she didn't approach him in fear when he reached out to her.
Their lives intersected through innocence and ignorance.
They became friends and stayed friends
Until his owner moved him away.
She hoped he'd find a new friend wherever he went.

A Haiku for Zebras

Black on white ripples
Against firm equine muscles –
Zebras on parade

Zebra Stripes

When God created humans
He made them every shade.
Some pink, some brown, some reddish,
Some yellow skinned He made.
And just to set examples
Of how things ought to be,
He used the skins of creatures
To show diversity.
With varied colors offered
And patterns of all kinds,
He set His marks to teach us
And to edify our minds.
Some are solid-colored creatures,
Some blotched, and some with dots,
Some striped in part or total,
Some with spots inside of spots!
My favorite is the zebra,
Its lesson plain to see.
Not black nor white, it's neither,
And it's both, so clear to me.
A special place for zebras
Is found within my heart.
Such harmony can fill the world,
If we will only start
To look beyond the skin tone
To the beating heart inside
Is the precious lesson we should learn
From the zebra's striped hide.

Cares and Fears

I thought it simple to forget my cares,
To let them go, like water through a chine.
Too late, I saw the ground then lost — acres
Washed away. Better then to build a niche,

And hide them there. From biggest to the least,
From elephants to microscopic fleas,
I bury them lest any of them steal
My peace of mind with presentations false.

Unbidden, they will seek to rule my life
With trickery and lies behind a veil.
If only I could lose them! I would lief
Go through my life without their message vile.

I fight them on each side as best I dare
And hold the gift of peace of mind more dear.

(Author's note: This is a "break the rules" sonnet with the rhymes replaced by anagram pairs.

Honorable Mention, Alabama State Poetry Society Award, "Break the Rules," NFSPS 2024

Bear in the Woods

Bear in the woods, fish in the stream.
Little girls play and big girls dream.
Stars in the sky, wind on the sea.
Once I had dreams of what I would be.
But my dreams blew away in the storms of life,
I've built new dreams on the rubble of strife.
Though not what I planned all those long years ago
These dreams I've achieved built a good life, and so
I thank God for the bears, the fish and the stars
The wind in the trees and His other wonders.
I thank Him for giving me the life I now know,
For letting me learn and letting me grow.
Bear in the woods, fish in the stream…
He's given me more than e'er I could dream.

The Herd

Trunks swaying with each ponderous step,
The elephants move through the trees.
They seek fresh water this day,
A quiet place to rest
And food to nourish
For young and old.
In time, they
Will move
On.

Thank You

I appreciate you taking this journey with me. Perhaps you've encountered an old friend in these pages or made a new one.

The animal world around us offers companionship, fun and beauty. Take time to enjoy the creatures in your world. They are gifts from God.

On the pages following, you'll find a list of my poetry work in print as well as an index of the poems by form.

You are cordially invited to visit my webpage, www.LOL4.net, to learn more about me and my work.

Blessings,

Mary Beth

Poetry Books by Mary Beth Magee

- Songs of Childhood, Echoes of Years
- Life and All: The Journey
- Grandpa's Mustache
- The World Through Tears
- Paw Prints on My Heart

Poetry Anthology Appearances by Mary Beth Magee

- Celebrating Mississippi – The Mississippi Poetry Society 85th Year Anthology
- Mississippi Poetry Journal 2018 – Contest Edition
- Southern Holidays (South Branch)
- Mississippi Poetry Journal 2022 – Contest Edition
- Forty Years – A Celebration (South Branch)
- Mississippi Poetry Journal 2023 – Contest Edition
- Mississippi Poetry Journal 2024 – Contest Edition
- National Federation of State Poetry Societies 2024 Encore— Contest Edition
- Mississippi Writers Guild-Coastal Chapter "Oasis of Light" anthology
- Picayune Writers Group 2024 Anthology "Felines and Phantoms"
- "Flights of Fantasy " - PagesPromotions.com fundraising anthology
- "Walt Whitman 205" commemorative anthology
- "Minute Musings" anthology
- "Gathering 2024" anthology
- Creative Minds Writers Group 2024 anthology

Index by Poetic Form

Form	Title	Page
Ekphrastic	Blue Dog Blues	8
	Draped in Pearls	30
	Multiple Personalities	13
	The Panther	24
Fibonacci	Dog Tales	5
Free Verse	A Cat Named Stu	20
	Boys and Dogs and James H Street	7
	Cougar Encounter	43
	Dragonflies	29
	Dragonfly Alibis	27
	Feathered Flood	36
	Fifty Words for Puppy	12
	Living with Nature	44
	Porch Dragon	49
	Ruby Wings	37
	Serpentine	51
	Spooky	54
	The Parsley Thief	32
	The Rescue	9
	The Symphony	47
	Zebra Stripes	57
Haiku	A Haiku for Puffins	38
	A Haiku for Zebras	56
Kelly Lune	Dinner Bell!	51
	Puppy Tails	10
Nonet	The Herd	60
Prose Poem	The Rope	50

Form	Title	Page
Rhymed	Alley, Alley, All in Free	18
	Bear in the Woods	59
	Disappearing Act	17
	Emerald Orbs	21
	Jacques Edmund	23
	Little Armadillo	48
	One Golden Horse	53
	Pelican Power	35
	Saddle Up!	52
	Sentinel	11
	Southern Beauty	46
	The Bookstore Cat	19
	The Clever Kitten	22
	The Visitor	28
Sonnet	Cares and Fears	58
	Puffins	39
	Puppy Ears	6
Trimeric	Butterflies	31

Index by Title

Title	Page
Alley, Alley, All in Free	18
Bear in the Woods	59
Blue Dog Blues	8
Bookstore Cat, The	19
Boys and Dogs and James H Street	7
Butterflies	31
Cares and Fears	58
Cat Named Stu, A	20
Clever Kitten, The	22
Cougar Encounter	43
Dinner Bell!	51
Disappearing Act	17
Dog Tales	5
Dragonflies	29
Dragonfly Alibis	27
Draped in Pearls	30
Emerald Orbs	21
Feathered Flood	36
Fifty Words for Puppy	12
Haiku for Puffins, A	38
Haiku for Zebras, A	56
Herd, The	60
Jacques Edmund	23
Little Armadillo	48
Living with Nature	44
Multiple Personalities	13
One Golden Horse	53
Panther, The	24
Parsley Thief, The	32

Title	Page
Pelican Power	35
Porch Dragon	49
Puffins	39
Puppy Ears	6
Puppy Tails	10
Rescue, The	9
Rope, The	50
Ruby Wings	37
Saddle Up!	52
Sentinel	11
Serpentine	51
Southern Beauty	46
Spooky	54
Symphony, The	47
Visitor, The	28
Zebra Stripes	57

www.ingramcontent.com/pod-product-compliance
Lightning Source LLC
Chambersburg PA
CBHW060351050426
42449CB00011B/2921